heartfelt ministering

Tools to Help You *Minister* in a Newer, Holier Way

CFI • An imprint of Cedar Fort, Inc.
Springville, Utah

ISBN 13: 978-1-4621-2274-5

Published by CFI, an imprint of Cedar Fort, Inc.
2373 W. 700 S., Springville, UT 84663
Distributed by Cedar Fort, Inc., www.cedarfort.com

Library of Congress Control Number: 2018952500

Cover design and interiors by Shawnda T. Craig
Cover design © 2018 Cedar Fort, Inc.
Edited by Nicole Terry and Kaitlin Barwick

Printed in the United States of America

10 9 8 7 6 5 4 3 2 1

Printed on acid-free paper

Contents

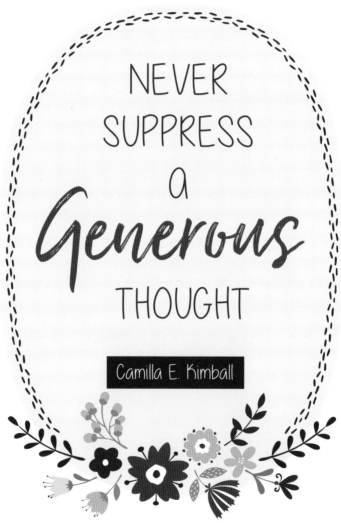

NEVER
SUPPRESS
a
Generous
THOUGHT

Camilla E. Kimball

Ministering That Matches the Message:
how to use this book

This book isn't intended to make your ministering mindless. Instead, we hope to inspire you to *act* and learn to minister entirely under the direction of the Holy Ghost through personal revelation. Use these cards and the ideas presented in the introduction as a springboard to help you take your ministering to a new level—the "newer, holier approach"[1] President Nelson envisioned when announcements were made about the new ministering program in the April 2018 General Conference.

The Savior ministered one by one, matching His message and His actions to the specific needs of those He served. Deep, heartfelt relationships aren't created with a simple birthday card, a quote about baptism, or a printed sentiment about the significance of Christmas, but they can begin there.

As you become closer to the people you minister to, you will get better at noticing what they need. You'll also get better at responding to specific needs. True ministering will require true friendship plus true charity, the pure love of Christ. That may take some time to develop, so in the meantime, *practice* receiving revelation.

Prayerfully use each of the quotations, ideas, and thoughts presented here as you develop confidence to act on every generous thought and first prompting the Spirit gives you.

How to use the quotations and tags in this book

- Text a digital version of a quote to someone you have been thinking about (visit www.lynnaeallred.com/HeartfeltMinistering to download).
- Write a quick note on the back of one of the cards and tuck it under the windshield wiper of a friend's car at church.
- Include a quote inside a thank-you card or a letter.

---

1. Russell M. Nelson, "Ministering," *Ensign*, May 2018.

- Tape it to your roommate's, child's, or spouse's mirror.
- Keep a couple in your car glove box, backpack, or purse to accompany any random act of kindness you perform.

Your persistent and genuine desire to truly develop friendships with those you serve will lead you to your knees. As you get into the habit of praying for those you serve, the Holy Ghost will begin to direct your efforts. Ideas and impressions will continue to come. You will "act on the first prompting,"[2] and you will grow into a friendship that will bless you and your family eternally.

How did the Savior minister?

If you want to be a disciple of Jesus Christ and minister to others as He did, it may be helpful to embark on a little research project. Who did the Savior minister to, and what did that look like?

While the Savior cleansed lepers and helped the blind to see, He also had enough insight into His friends' needs to know when they needed rest (see Mark 6:31–34), when they needed to eat (Luke 9:13), and when they were afraid (Matthew 8:25–26). He didn't minister simply to those who were lame, halt, stricken with palsy, and deaf. He sat at tables with people who were unpopular (Mark 2:15–16), wept with friends and family who were hurting physically and emotionally (John 11:32–36), and called down ministering angels to encircle children in love (3 Nephi 17:21–25).

While your assigned ministry includes specific individuals or geographic areas, the opportunities to minister are not always going to fall within those strict boundaries. Like the woman of Canaan who came to Christ and said, "Lord, help me," there will be hundreds of people outside of your jurisdiction who cross your path and will need the care of the Savior in their lives (Matthew 15:25). You are the instrument He will use to bless them. Ministering cannot be restricted just to those we are *assigned* to watch over. It has to extend beyond ward and branch boundaries.

It will also extend beyond members of the Church because ministering to others is an extension of our love for the Savior. "I want others to feel what I feel as a consequence of my having felt the effects of the Atonement in my own life," said a young single adult sister. "My burdens have been lightened because I have felt His forgiveness and His mercy. I want to share the beauty in my life that has been the result of my participation in the Atonement."

---

2. Ronald A. Rasband, "Let the Holy Spirit Guide," *Ensign*, May 2017.

❋ What do you want me to do today?

At the May 2018 BYU Women's Conference, Sister Sharon Eubank shared an example of how she manages to do what the Lord wants her to do:

"I know this isn't unique to me, but sometimes I'm so pressed with everything I have to do that I often don't even know what the priority is. I have started asking the Lord every morning, 'What is one thing you want me to do today?'"

". . . I had no idea how creative the Spirit can be! Some of my 'one' things have been making a phone call, teaching kids to play Yahtzee, listening to a forgetful friend tell stories I've already heard, and once it was taking a nap."

As you study the Savior's ministry, try an experiment similar to Sister Eubank's. Keep your ministering journal near the location where you kneel to say your personal prayers. Each morning, write one thing you feel inspired to do. Revisit your list at the end of the day. As you pray, express gratitude for the experiences you had as a result of following that prompting.

❋ Creating Common Ground and Real Friendships

How do you break the ice and start a friendship? The first step is taking the first step. Sometimes, especially if you tend to be more introverted yourself, the easiest way to do this is in a small group. What ideas will give you the opportunity to rub shoulders with someone you minister to in a more relaxed, fun-loving atmosphere? Learn what the individual interests are for those you serve, and build activities around those. If you restore vintage cars, love Mexican cuisine, or happen to be a terrific sushi chef, you can build a friendship around your unique talents or skills.

Maybe a group date to a matinee play with all of the widows in your ward could involve one of your ministering sisters and help ease her loneliness. Or, organize a "Lunch Serve" project with several sisters in your ward and work on a humanitarian service project while you visit over chicken salad sandwiches.

What about a ministering group of two? "I'm an introvert, so while I go to ward socials, that's not how I connect," one brother told me. "I connect by walking up the road and helping my neighbor irrigate his garden or hang his Christmas lights." One of the blessings of ministering is that it opens up more flexible methods of forming friendships. Everything "counts," and no one is a project any more. We can be motivated purely out of caring, concern, and hope—hope that we will feel less isolated ourselves as we try to befriend others.

It's fun to drop off a plate of warm cookies, but what if you gathered the families you minister to for a cookie swap or a Sunday evening hymn sing-along instead?

Invite your new friends to play board games, go on a double date, visit the temple, or enjoy a chocolate fondue night with you. As those first slightly awkward moments meld into more relaxed conversations, you will learn more about those you serve, and eventually, you'll be comfortable giving more personalized service. You'll see specific needs and will respond to those needs with love and creativity.

Together, We Are Enough:
creative ways the group can minister to the one

Soon after the new ministering program was introduced, I received a phone call from a ward member. His family had been through a difficult stretch of adversity, including a serious illness that nearly took the life of one of his missionary sons, leaving him partially paralyzed. Every single member of this stalwart family experienced a challenge of one kind or another. Taken alone, they would have been manageable, but coming one on top of another, the steady stream of hardship was taking its toll.

Usual expressions of sympathy—meals and casseroles, plates of goodies, expressions of concern, adding names to temple prayer roll—were all much appreciated, and the family constantly expressed gratitude. But after yet another hospitalization for their missionary son, this thoughtful father called to tell me he had been pondering what his family needed most. "My wife spends as much time as she can at the hospital, and meals are appreciated, but what she really loves is fresh-cut flowers. Could you let the sisters know we are grateful for our overflowing refrigerator and if they would like to give her a lift, a small bouquet of anything from their garden would be much appreciated?"

There were several things I learned from this exchange.

First, this brother's first concern was for his sweetheart and her comfort. Second, he had to set aside his own pride in order to make a request. Third, instead of complaining about what we were doing too much of, he opened another door we didn't know existed. His honesty allowed us to do something specific that would be truly helpful to meet his wife's *specific* needs.

His request prompted a "plan to act". Relief Society sisters agreed to deliver one or two stems of flowers from their own gardens on a specific day of the week to one of our young, new mothers who is a talented floral designer.

On the appointed day, the doorbell rang several times with deliveries of peonies, bleeding heart sprigs, store-bought lilies, extra vases, and more. One sister who was out of town gave instructions for someone to go to her home to cut several of her dark purple iris. No one had enough flowers in bloom to provide for an entire bouquet, but combined together, there were enough for a large, attractive arrangement.

I love this example of ministering because it represents the power of a group effort. Sometimes problems are so intractable and large that it's beyond the ability of a single individual or companionship to manage them alone. Coming up with an idea that allows a group to serve together meets the needs of both givers and recipients.

This is where the power of councils comes in.

During your ministering interview, you have the opportunity to share your ideas and concerns with the Relief Society presidency or elders quorum presidency and to "give an accounting" of your service and share what you have done to watch over, love, and comfort those you serve.

This makes it possible for you to be sure problems you can't tackle alone are addressed. (Remember that sensitive or confidential information should be reported directly to the Relief Society president or elders quorum president.)

Here are some examples of council-based ministering I've seen recently:

- An elders quorum worked together to repair a dangerously unstable backyard wood staircase and deck for a single mother in the ward.
- Ward members joined in a community-wide cleanup effort (which included members of many faiths) to pick up springtime tree and shrub trimmings and haul them to a yard waste recycling facility.
- Knowing of a job opening to assist a disabled ward member, a ministering sister contacted her Relief Society president. Information was forwarded to the stake Relief Society president, who shared the job opening with members of the stake via ward Relief Society presidents and employment specialists. In another instance, an urgent need for a stake member to find an apartment was broadcast the same way.
- A sister was admitted to the hospital. She is the caregiver for her husband, who suffers from Alzheimer's disease and also for her daughter with special needs.

Her ministering sisters helped organize shifts for ward members to be in the home to provide care for them until she was well enough to return home.
- Young women were mobilized to help unbox and repackage products for a sister's home-based business when she became too ill to do it herself.

In the past, you've known these efforts as "service projects." They are often organized and run by members of quorum and auxiliary presidencies. But now, as a ministering brother or sister, you have been charged by the prophet to take a "newer, holier approach." You have insight a presidency member lacks about *specific* needs of the families you serve. As you report these needs during your ministering interview, you engage the efforts of a ward council. In turn, the council may engage you as a member of the larger group that works together to solve the problem.

Finally, it's critical to remember that beyond providing for temporal needs, the greater purpose of ministering is to exalt families. President Russell M. Nelson summed up the true purpose of ministering this way: "Our message to the world is simple and sincere: we invite all of God's children on both sides of the veil to come unto their Savior, receive the blessings of the holy temple, have enduring joy, and qualify for eternal life."[3]

Detachable, Deliverable Quotes

While the *first* step is to seek the guidance of the Spirit, the following quote cards are provided as an *accessory* to your ministering efforts. They cannot replace ministering, but they may help simplify and encourage your inspired efforts.
For example, here are some ideas for using the first four cards:

Scatter Sunshine

- Hang the card from a ribbon tied around a brightly colored bouquet of flowers.
- Attach the card to a yellow gift bag. Fill the bag with items that are packaged completely in yellow-hued packaging, such as peanut M&M's, Lemon-flavored candy, yellow nail polish, lip balm, etc.
- Attach the card to a packet or envelope that holds flower seeds.
- Hand the card to one of the youth speakers after sacrament meeting with a note on the back thanking them for a specific thought that touched you.

---

3. Russell M. Nelson, "Let Us All Press On," *Ensign*, May 2018.

- Download the digital image of the card (see www.lynnaeallred.com /HeartfeltMinistering). Text the photo to one of your ministering sisters along with a compliment. Encourage them to "scatter sunshine" by sending the photo and a compliment on to someone else.

"Enduring to the end is definitely not a do-it-yourself project."

- Call your ministering sister/brother and ask if he or she could help you with a small DIY project. Give the card to him or her at the end of the day as a thank you card.
- Think of the hobbies your ministering sister or ministering brother enjoys. Add the card to a package of paint brushes, quilting fat quarters, a DIY craft kit, or any other useful hobby supplies.
- Download a digital version and email it to a friend along with a DIY recipe that looks delicious to you.
- Write a letter to a missionary and mail the card along with it.

"The difficulties which come to us present us with the real test of our ability to endure."

- Remove the wrapper from a favorite candy bar and replace it with a copy of the card. Deliver it to someone who is in poor health.
- Wrap the card up in an especially soft blanket to give to someone who has just lost a spouse or family member.
- If a member of one of your ministering families is critically ill or has been injured, plan a trip to the hospital for a brief visit. Decide at the end of your
- visit whether it is appropriate to give them the card. The card isn't as important as your visit.
- Mail the card to someone you love who resides in a care center along with a handwritten note of encouragement and love.

"Without hard work, nothing grows but weeds."

- Call someone you minister to and offer to help them with a yard-care project such as pruning roses, weeding, installing or repairing a sprinkling system, repairing or painting a deck, laying sod, spreading mulch, planting bedding plants, fertilizing the lawn, or putting garden seeds in. If you are a property owner, outside work is almost endless, and it can be fun to work side by side with someone as you chat.

- Hire the son or daughter of the family you minister to as an assistant for a project you are working on. At the end of the workday, wrap the card around a can or bottle of their favorite cold drink and deliver it along with payment for services rendered.
- Put the card on the table with the next tip you leave at a restaurant, along with a note of appreciation to the server.
- Attend a musical recital of one of the youth in the family you minister to. Attach the card to a gift certificate to a local music store where the individual can purchase some sheet music.
- Attend a sporting event of one of the youth in the family you minister to. Congratulate them for their great effort with a note on the back of the card that you leave taped to the window of their car.
- Share something from your garden or the farmer's market you know your friend will enjoy. Attach the card to the delivery bag with some colorful ribbon or some twine.
- Make a hand-painted pot or repurpose a unique container you have on hand, and plant one or two culinary herbs to grow indoors. Use decorative handwriting to write the name of the herb on the back of the card, then attach the card to a stick and place it into the pot prior to delivery.
- Mail the card to a university student, along with a letter from you.

scatter sunshine
(Hymns, no. 230)

scatter sunshine
(Hymns, no. 230)

ENDURING
TO THE END
is definitely
not a
do-it-yourself
project.

—L. Tom Perry

ENDURING
TO THE END
is definitely
not a
do-it-yourself
project.

—L. Tom Perry

L. Tom Perry, "The Gospel of Jesus Christ," *Ensign*, May 2008.

THE DIFFICULTIES WHICH COME TO US
PRESENT US WITH THE REAL TEST
OF OUR ABILITY TO ENDURE.
A FUNDAMENTAL QUESTION REMAINS
TO BE ANSWERED BY EACH OF US:

SHALL I FALTER, OR SHALL I FINISH?

—THOMAS S. MONSON

THE DIFFICULTIES WHICH COME TO US
PRESENT US WITH THE REAL TEST
OF OUR ABILITY TO ENDURE.
A FUNDAMENTAL QUESTION REMAINS
TO BE ANSWERED BY EACH OF US:

SHALL I FALTER, OR SHALL I FINISH?

—THOMAS S. MONSON

Thomas S. Monson, "I Will Not Fail Thee, nor Forsake Thee," *Ensign*, November 2013.

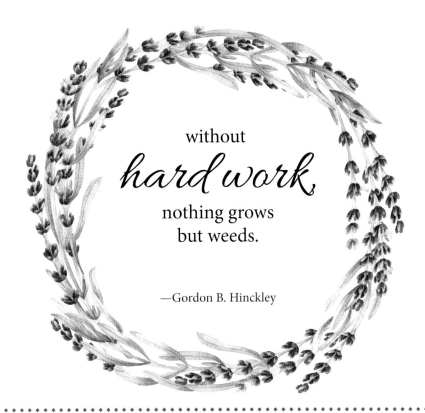

without
hard work,
nothing grows
but weeds.

—Gordon B. Hinckley

without
hard work,
nothing grows
but weeds.

—Gordon B. Hinckley

do what is

RIGHT;

let the consequence follow.

(*HYMNS*, NO. 237)

·· ❖ ··

do what is

RIGHT;

let the consequence follow.

(*HYMNS*, NO. 237)

WE OURSELVES FEEL THAT WHAT WE ARE DOING IS JUST A DROP IN THE OCEAN. BUT IF THE DROP WAS NOT IN THE OCEAN, I THINK THE OCEAN WOULD BE LESS BECAUSE OF THE MISSING DROP.

—MOTHER TERESA

WE OURSELVES FEEL THAT WHAT WE ARE DOING IS JUST A DROP IN THE OCEAN. BUT IF THE DROP WAS NOT IN THE OCEAN, I THINK THE OCEAN WOULD BE LESS BECAUSE OF THE MISSING DROP.

—MOTHER TERESA

Mother Teresa, as quoted in *Mother Teresa's Reaching Out In Love—Stories Told by Mother Teresa*, compiled and edited by Edward Le Joly and Jaya Chaliha (New York: Barnes and Noble, 2002), 122.

Let your companions
be such as yourself,
or superior;
for the worth of a man
will always be ruled by
that of his company.

—Lord Admiral Cuthbert Collingwood

Let your companions
be such as yourself,
or superior;
for the worth of a man
will always be ruled by
that of his company.

—Lord Admiral Cuthbert Collingwood

Cuthbert Collingwood, from a letter to Mr. Lane, November 7, 1787,
as quoted in *American Journal of Education* 1, no. 2 (March 1830): 89.

COMPARISON IS THE THIEF OF *joy*

—THEODORE ROOSEVELT

•••

COMPARISON IS THE THIEF OF *joy*

—THEODORE ROOSEVELT

Theodore Roosevelt, as quoted in Kenneth B. Cooper, Nels Gustafson, and Joseph G. Salah, *Becoming a Great School* (New York: Rowman & Littlefield Education, 2014), ix.

Where there is **discord**,
may we bring *harmony*.

Where there is **error**,
may we bring *truth*.

Where there is **doubt**,
may we bring *faith*.

And where there is **despair**,
may we bring *hope*.

—Margaret Thatcher

Where there is **discord**,
may we bring *harmony*.

Where there is **error**,
may we bring *truth*.

Where there is **doubt**,
may we bring *faith*.

And where there is **despair**,
may we bring *hope*.

—Margaret Thatcher

Margaret Thatcher, as quoted in "Remarks on Becoming Prime Minister (St. Francis's Prayer)," Margaret Thatcher Foundation, accessed June 13, 2018, https://www.margaretthatcher.org/document/104078.

WELCOME
THE TASK
THAT MAKES
YOU
GO BEYOND
YOURSELF

—LOUISE YATES ROBISON

WELCOME
THE TASK
THAT MAKES
YOU
GO BEYOND
YOURSELF

—LOUISE YATES ROBISON

To be good,
and to do good,
is the whole
duty of man
comprised in a few
words.

-Abigail Adams

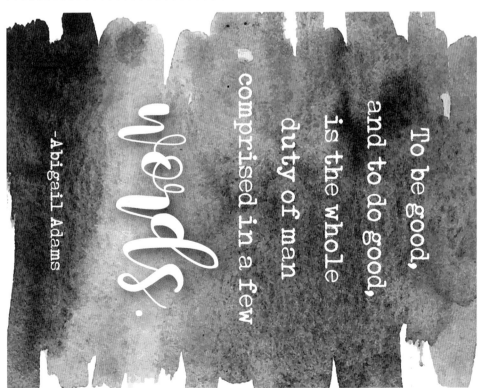

To be good,
and to do good,
is the whole
duty of man
comprised in a few
words.

-Abigail Adams

Abigail Adams, letter to Elizabeth Shaw (1784), quoted in David McCullough,
John Adams (New York: Simon and Schuster, 2001), 310.

DISCIPLESHIP TO THE SAVIOR IS THE PRESCRIBED

pathway of joy.

—Fran C. Hafen

• •

DISCIPLESHIP TO THE SAVIOR IS THE PRESCRIBED

pathway of joy.

—Fran C. Hafen

Fran C. Hafen, *Rejoice: How to Find and Keep the Savior's Joy*
(Springville, UT: Cedar Fort, 2017), 111.

NEVER SUPPRESS a Generous THOUGHT

Camilla E. Kimball

NEVER SUPPRESS a Generous THOUGHT

Camilla E. Kimball

Camilla Kimball, as quoted in Julie B. Beck, "Relief Society:
A Sacred Work," *Ensign*, November 2009.

Decisions
Determine
Destiny

Thomas S. Monson

Decisions
Determine
Destiny

Thomas S. Monson

Thomas S. Monson, "Decisions Determine Destiny" (Brigham Young
University devotional, November 6, 2005), speeches.byu.edu.

"The world is divided into people who do things - and - people who get the credit. Try, if you can, to belong to the first class. There's far less competition."

—Dwight Whitney Morrow

"The world is divided into people who do things - and - people who get the credit. Try, if you can, to belong to the first class. There's far less competition."

—Dwight Whitney Morrow

Dwight Whitney Morrow, from a letter to his son, as quoted in Harold Nicolson, *Dwight Morrow* (New York: Harcourt, Brace and Company, 1935), 52.

I don't have to be perfect for the Lord to use me.

—Sally Marks

I don't have to be perfect for the Lord to use me.

—Sally Marks

Sally Marks, "I'm a Mormon, Addict Caretaker, and a Voice for the Homeless," LDS Media Library, https://www .lds.org/media-library/video/2010-06-2008-im-a-mormon-addict-caretaker-and-voice-for-the-homeless.

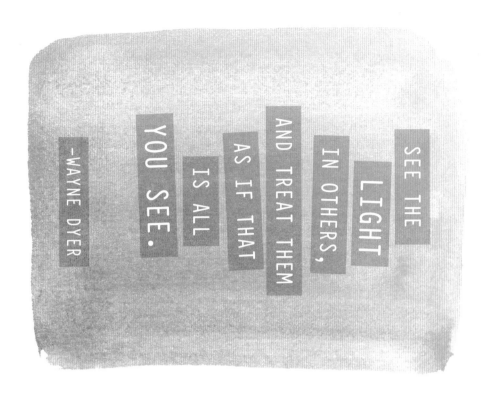

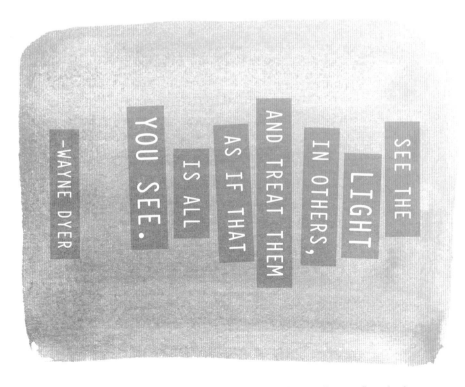

Wayne Dyer, "See the light in others, and treat them as if that is all you see," Facebook post, November 21, 2011, https://www.facebook.com/drwaynedyer/posts/10150410935516030.

THE "NEXT ORDINANCE":
saving ordinances through your encouragement and support

Speaking to the Young Men in the October 2012 General Conference, Gary E. Stevenson, who was then serving as the Presiding Bishop, encouraged all young men to receive their "next ordinance" at the proper age and ultimately receive the Melchizedek Priesthood.[4] What can you do to help those you minister to receive their own "next ordinance"?

President Russell M. Nelson emphasized our responsibility to focus our ministering efforts on helping others achieve exaltation. "I invite you to inspire members to keep their covenants, fast and pray, study the scriptures, worship in the temple, and serve with faith as men and women of God. We can help all to see with the eye of faith that obedience and righteousness will draw them closer to Jesus Christ, allow them to enjoy the companionship of the Holy Ghost, and experience joy in life!"[5]

First, it's helpful to review the list of saving ordinances. These include
- Baptism
- Confirmation
- Ordination to the Melchizedek Priesthood (for men)
- Temple endowment
- Marriage sealing

Additional ordinances, including blessing of babies and the sacrament ordinance can be considered. Is there anyone you minister to who may benefit from a priesthood blessing?

Write the names of those you serve (don't forget to include their family members!). What is the next ordinance for each of them?

---

4. Gary E. Stephenson, "Be Valiant in Courage, Strength, and Activity," *Ensign*, November 2012.
5. Russell M. Nelson, "Ministering with the Power and Authority of God," *Ensign*, May 2018.

As you fast and pray about these names, what impressions and ideas come to you for ways you can help each of them prepare to progress? Can they identify barriers that are stopping or hindering their progress? What can you do to help eliminate those barriers? If they are progressing, how can you show support? Here is a list of ideas to get you started:

Baptism and Confirmation

For Children:
- Give a gift subscription to the *Friend* magazine.
- Invite the whole family to a special baptism Family Home Evening.
- Deliver a new white towel the child can use at his or her baptism with the note from page 53 of this book.
- Attend the baptism and confirmation.

For Youth and Adults:
- Sit in on missionary discussions and offer encouragement.
- Give a gift subscription to the *New Era, Ensign,* or *Liahona* magazines.
- Offer to help locate appropriate white clothing for the baptism ordinance.
- Think of a thoughtful gift you can give to help them remember the day, such as a journal with a special note or favorite scripture attached.
- Attend the baptism and confirmation.

Priesthood Ordinations for Young Men and Prospective Elders

As a ministering brother who serves a family with a prospective elder, it can be helpful to think about things you can do befriend and show Christlike love, whether he's a seventeen-year-old who is eagerly preparing for a mission, or whether he's a returning member who has never been ordained.

In the April 2018 General Conference, President Nelson shared the story of a ci-gar-smoking Church member who had been ordained and sealed but was no longer active. President Nelson became friends with this brother by first taking a sincere interest in his amateur radio hobby.[6]

Elder Ned B. Roueché of the Second Quorum of the Seventy was activated by the same method. A sister in his ward, taking note of his interest in ballroom dance, invited him to perform a dance floor show number at an MIA activity. When he arrived, he realized

---

6. Ibid.

he and his dance partner weren't *on* the program. They *were* the program. "It was an exciting experience, and I thoroughly enjoyed the evening," wrote Elder Roueché.

"The following Sunday morning, I decided to go to church in our ward for the first time since I was ordained a deacon. At that time, none of my family was active. I found people who welcomed me warmly, and they demonstrated a genuine friendship and caring. These experiences started me on the road to activity and service in the Church that has been a joy to me throughout the years."[7]

Showing a young man he is accepted and needed may be one of the best ways to be-friend him. Does he have an interest in cars, cartooning, computers, chocolate ice cream? Do you have a hobby you could introduce to him? My grandfather was inactive for much of my father's young adult life, but other adults took an interest in Dad's progress. His Uncle Verl collected electric trains and also had a pilot's license. My Dad recalls trying to sell the most raffle tickets to a ward dinner so he could win the coveted plane ride with Uncle Verl. (Raising funds for ward building projects was common in those days). Think of ways you can appropriately show kindness to a prospective elder, whether he's seventeen or seventy-seven.

- Ask him to help you wash and detail a vehicle for one of the widows in the ward or branch. Show your admiration for his vehicle if he has one he's proud of.
- Ask him what his favorite dessert or candy bar is, and deliver one as a congratulations for any special achievement, or for no reason at all.
- Write a note of appreciation with specific details about what you learned from him when he was the youth speaker in sacrament meeting.
- Ask him if he would be willing to help you with a project in the yard. Talking as you work side by side can be much less intimidating than a face-to-face conversation.

Temple Endowment

The temple endowment is a sacred experience, and whether preparation for the endowment comes prior to mission service, as part of a marriage sealing, or is received later in life, it is an opportunity for a ministering brother or sister to show support and love.

- Invite those preparing for an endowment to attend the temple with you to perform baptisms for the dead.
- A photograph of the temple to keep in the home may be an appropriate gift for someone preparing to attend the temple.

---

7. Ned B. Roueché, "Fellowshipping," *Ensign*, May 1999.

- If a missionary is receiving an endowment as part of a mission call, a miniture desk flag representing the state, province, or country where he or she will be serving along with a small desk holder can be a fun gift to deliver with a note of best wishes.

Temple Sealing

One afternoon, I was visiting with an older sister in our ward whose husband had become an active member of the Church long after he retired. She shared that she had come home from work late on November 9, 1998, to find her husband, Bryant, watching television coverage of the fall of the Berlin Wall.

"Elaine, will you look at that! Those people have waited more than twenty-eight years to be able to have the privilege of seeing their family members on the other side of that wall. They've waited so long to be connected to their families!"

"Yes," Elaine responded, "and I've waited even longer than that."

Stunned, her husband realized what she was referring to. She had waited for all of their married life for him to become worthy to attend the temple so they could be sealed to their family members, including a son who had died in the Vietnam War. Bryant began the process of preparing to attend the temple that very evening and they were sealed several months later.

Is one of the family members you minister to waiting for the opportunity to be sealed? Ministering brothers and sisters have significant influence helping individuals, couples, or entire families prepare for this ordinance.

- A Christmas ornament representing the temple can be a beautiful expression of hope and support.
- Offer to attend a temple preparation class along with the individual or couple you minister to.
- Be a good example by attending the temple yourself and sharing some of your best experiences.
- Visit the temple grounds with your friend just to walk around together and enjoy the sacred spirit.
- If you minister to a part-member family, recognize that attending the temple alone may be a lonely experience for the brother or sister you serve. Offer to attend with them on a regular basis.

For I have given you an example,
that ye should do as I have done to you.

John 13:15

Congratulations

on your **BAPTISM &**
CONFIRMATION!

- -

For I have given you an example,
that ye should do as I have done to you.

John 13:15

Congratulations

on your **BAPTISM &**
CONFIRMATION!

HIS LOVE IS GREAT;

HE DIED FOR US.

SHALL WE UNGRATEFUL BE,

SINCE HE HAS MARKED

A ROAD TO BLISS

AND SAID,

"COME, FOLLOW ME"?

HYMNS, NO. 65

HIS LOVE IS GREAT;

HE DIED FOR US.

SHALL WE UNGRATEFUL BE,

SINCE HE HAS MARKED

A ROAD TO BLISS

AND SAID,

"COME, FOLLOW ME"?

HYMNS, NO. 65

"A happy marriage is not so much a matter of romance as it is an anxious concern for the **comfort** and **well-being** of one's companion."

—Gordon B. Hinckley

"A happy marriage is not so much a matter of romance as it is an anxious concern for the **comfort** and **well-being** of one's companion."

—Gordon B. Hinckley

Gordon B. Hinckley, "What God Hath Joined Together," *Ensign*, May 1991.

"*I have often said one of the* greatest secrets of missionary work is work! *If a missionary works,* he will get the Spirit*; if he gets the Spirit,* he will teach by the Spirit*; and if he teaches by the Spirit,* he will touch the hearts of the people and he will be happy*. Work, Work, Work— there is no satisfactory substitute, especailly in missionary work.*"

—Ezra Taft Benson

"*I have often said one of the* greatest secrets of missionary work is work! *If a missionary works,* he will get the Spirit*; if he gets the Spirit,* he will teach by the Spirit*; and if he teaches by the Spirit,* he will touch the hearts of the people and he will be happy*. Work, Work, Work— there is no satisfactory substitute, especailly in missionary work.*"

—Ezra Taft Benson

Ezra Taft Benson, "Keys to Successful Member Missionary Work," *Ensign*, September 1990.

THE ENDOWMENT IS A BESTOWAL OF HEAVENLY POWER AND KNOWLEDGE. IT IS LITERALLY A "GIFT."

THE ENDOWMENT IS A BESTOWAL OF HEAVENLY POWER AND KNOWLEDGE. IT IS LITERALLY A "GIFT."

"Endowed from on High," LDS.org, https://www.lds.org/youth/article/endowed-from-on-high.

Holidays and Celebrations

A holiday is a great excuse to send a text, plan an event, hold a celebration, or drop off a gift. It's a nice time to let someone know you are thinking of them. And the best thing about a holiday is that many of them have been created for the express purpose of being grateful—grateful for relationships, grateful for freedoms, grateful for sacrifices made by others to make our own lives better.

Notes from the following pages will help you acknowledge reasons to celebrate and give you another point of contact with those you minister to. "By small and simple things are great things brought to pass" (Alma 37:6).

There's more good news about events and celebrations. If you are too busy to make a contact on January 1 to wish someone Happy New Year, move on to January 2 and celebrate National Cream Puff Day instead. Visit nationaldaycalendar.com for a list of hundreds of national US holidays you didn't know existed. These can become fun, creative excuses to make contact—for no reason at all except that you are thinking of someone and want them to know.

For reference, here are a few events that may lend themselves especially well to your own "led by the spirit, flexible, and customized"[8] ministering efforts:

- January 9 – National Law Enforcement Appreciation Day
- Second Sunday in January – National Sunday Supper Day
- January 21 – National Hugging Day
- February 7 – National Send a Card to a Friend Day
- February 11 – National Shut-In Visitation Day
- February 16 – National Caregivers' Day
- February 17 – National Random Acts of Kindness Day
- March 3 – National Soup It Forward Day
- March 21 – National Single Parent Day
- First Wednesday in April – National Walking Day

8. Sharon Eubank, in Marianne Holman Prescott, "Relief Society General Presidency Shares Insights about the Call to Minister," *Church News*, May 4, 2018, https://www.lds.org/church/news/relief-society-general-presidency-shares-insights-about-the-call-to-minister.

- April 10 – National Siblings Day
- April 30 – National Hairstylist Appreciation Day
- May 6 – National Infertility Survival Day
- May 8 – National Teacher Appreciation Day
- Second Sunday in May – Mother's Day
- May 18 – National Visit Your Relatives Day
- May 31 – National Smile Day
- June 1 – National Say Something Nice Day
- June 13 – National Weed Your Garden Day
- Third Sunday in June – Father's Day
- July 11 – National Cheer Up the Lonely Day
- September 9 – National Grandparents' Day
- Fourth Saturday in October – National Make a Difference Day
- November – National World Kindness Week
- November – National Hunger and Homeless Awareness Week
- December 1–25 – #LightTheWorld Initiative begins
  (see www.mormon.org/christmas)

Happy Birthday!

Just think how many years now the world has been enjoying you!

Happy Birthday!

Just think how many years now the world has been enjoying you!

BiRTHDaY

(noun) :

Nature's way of telling us
it's time to eat cake!

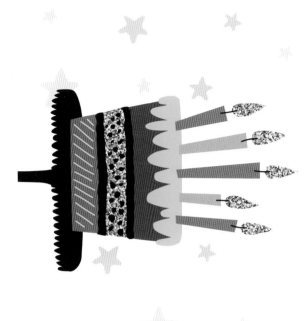

BiRTHDaY

(noun) :

Nature's way of telling us
it's time to eat cake!

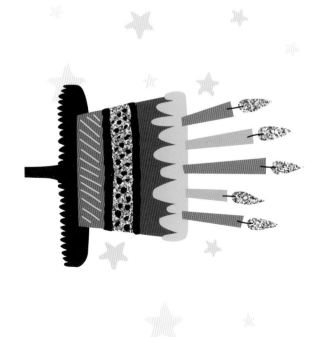

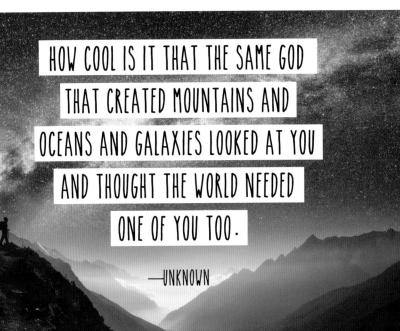

HOW COOL IS IT THAT THE SAME GOD THAT CREATED MOUNTAINS AND OCEANS AND GALAXIES LOOKED AT YOU AND THOUGHT THE WORLD NEEDED ONE OF YOU TOO.

—UNKNOWN

· ·

HOW COOL IS IT THAT THE SAME GOD THAT CREATED MOUNTAINS AND OCEANS AND GALAXIES LOOKED AT YOU AND THOUGHT THE WORLD NEEDED ONE OF YOU TOO.

—UNKNOWN

Romance

is created when you combine

EQUAL PARTS

WONDER & AFFECTION.

Love

Add

IS CREATED WHEN YOU

EMPATHY, CONCERN, AND SACRIFICE.

L. Allred

Romance

is created when you combine

EQUAL PARTS

WONDER & AFFECTION.

Love

Add

IS CREATED WHEN YOU

EMPATHY, CONCERN, AND SACRIFICE.

L. Allred

YOU HAVE A **NEW** ADDITION
IN THE HOUSE.
BET YOU ARE SO **EXCITED** ABOUT
THIS **NEW BABY** YOU CAN HARDLY
ᶻᶻᶻ **SLEEP!** ᶻᶻᶻ
CONGRATULATIONS!

YOU HAVE A **NEW** ADDITION
IN THE HOUSE.
BET YOU ARE SO **EXCITED** ABOUT
THIS **NEW BABY** YOU CAN HARDLY
ᶻᶻᶻ **SLEEP!** ᶻᶻᶻ
CONGRATULATIONS!

NATIONAL
POPCORN
DAY

JANUARY 19

**IT'S A GOOD THING I HAD THIS ON HAND
TO HELP YOU CELEBRATE PROPERLY!**

NATIONAL
POPCORN
DAY

JANUARY 19

**IT'S A GOOD THING I HAD THIS ON HAND
TO HELP YOU CELEBRATE PROPERLY!**

" *Love* DOESN'T MAKE THE WORLD GO ROUND.
Love IS WHAT MAKES THE RIDE *worthwhile*. "

-FRANKLIN P. JONES

" *Love* DOESN'T MAKE THE WORLD GO ROUND.
Love IS WHAT MAKES THE RIDE *worthwhile*. "

-FRANKLIN P. JONES

Franklin P. Jones, as quoted in Tracy Friesen, *Ride the Waves* (Victoria, BC: FriesenPress, 2013), 131.

MARCH 3
NATIONAL SOUP IT FORWARD DAY

Here's
passing
on warmth,
kindness,
and friendship
to someone
who constantly
shares it
with others.

MARCH 3
NATIONAL SOUP IT FORWARD DAY

Here's
passing
on warmth,
kindness,
and friendship
to someone
who constantly
shares it
with others.

—

"Be faithful and diligent in
keeping the commandments of
God, and I will encircle thee in the
arms of my love."
(D&C 6:20)

· ·

"Be faithful and diligent in
keeping the commandments of
God, and I will encircle thee in the
arms of my love."
(D&C 6:20)

PLEASE ACCEPT
OUR DEEPEST

sympathies.

OUR THOUGHTS
AND PRAYERS
ARE WITH YOU.

PLEASE ACCEPT
OUR DEEPEST

sympathies.

OUR THOUGHTS
AND PRAYERS
ARE WITH YOU.

· NATIONAL ·
GARDENING DAY

APRIL 14

HERE'S SOMETHING
TO GIVE YOUR GREEN
THUMB A WORKOUT.

· NATIONAL ·
GARDENING DAY

APRIL 14

HERE'S SOMETHING
TO GIVE YOUR GREEN
THUMB A WORKOUT.

"The loveliest masterpiece of the Heart of God is the Heart of a Mother."

—St. Therese of Lisieux

"The loveliest masterpiece of the Heart of God is the Heart of a Mother."

—St. Therese of Lisieux

St. Therese of Lisieux, as quoted in "The Heart of a Mother," Society of the Little Flower, May 10, 2018, https://blog.littleflower.org/st-therese-daily-devotional/heart-mother.

THERE IS

NOTHING BETTER

THAN A FRIEND,

UNLESS

IT IS A FRIEND

WHO HAS

CHOCOLATE.

♥

—UNKNOWN

THERE IS

NOTHING BETTER

THAN A FRIEND,

UNLESS

IT IS A FRIEND

WHO HAS

CHOCOLATE.

♥

—UNKNOWN

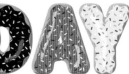

NATIONAL

DONUT DAY

is coming up on June 1, and I didn't
want you to have to celebrate alone.

ENJOY A DONUT ON ME!

✦ ✦

NATIONAL

DONUT DAY

is coming up on June 1, and I didn't
want you to have to celebrate alone.

ENJOY A DONUT ON ME!

THANKFUL
FOR OUR
FREEDOM
HAVE A
WONDERFUL
4TH OF JULY

THANKFUL
FOR OUR
FREEDOM
HAVE A
WONDERFUL
4TH OF JULY

NATIONAL **WAFFLE** DAY
IS AUGUST 24TH

I DIDN'T WANT YOU TO BE UNPREPARED!

NATIONAL **WAFFLE** DAY
IS AUGUST 24TH

I DIDN'T WANT YOU TO BE UNPREPARED!

NATIONAL HOMEMADE
COOKIES DAY
IS OCTOBER 1ST

GOOD THING WE BOOKEND
THE WHOLE MONTH WITH *sugar.*

NATIONAL HOMEMADE
COOKIES DAY
IS OCTOBER 1ST

GOOD THING WE BOOKEND
THE WHOLE MONTH WITH *sugar.*

Thankfulness is
MEASURED
BY THE NUMBER OF OUR WORDS

Gratitude is
MEASURED
BY THE NATURE OF OUR ACTIONS

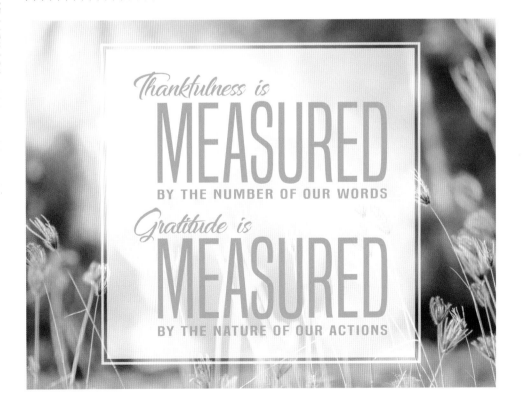

Thankfulness is
MEASURED
BY THE NUMBER OF OUR WORDS

Gratitude is
MEASURED
BY THE NATURE OF OUR ACTIONS

George Crabb, *Crabb's English Synomes* (New York: Grosset & Dunlap and Harper & Brothers, 1917), 671.

It's not what's
under the tree that

MATTERS

it's who is gathered
around it.

It's not what's
under the tree that

MATTERS

it's who is gathered
around it.

Blessed
are those who can
Give
without remembering &
Recieve
without forgetting

ELIZABETH BIBESCO

Blessed
are those who can
Give
without remembering &
Recieve
without forgetting

ELIZABETH BIBESCO

Adapted from Elizabeth Bibesco, *Haven* (London: James Barrie, 1951).

Practical "Plan to Act" Gift Tags

Here are some fun ideas for inexpensive gifts that will help encourage spiritual and temporal preparedness. You'll find gift tags you can attach to your preparedness gift. Blank gift tags are included so you can come up with your own creative preparedness ideas.

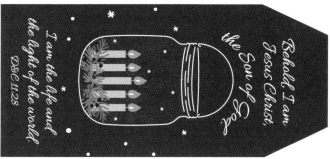

Christmas Celebration—Suggested gift: A Christmas Candle (A candle you can light every night in December to remind you of the Savior, who is the "Light of the World.")

Emergency Water Storage—Suggested gift: A
gallon of bottled water or a case of water bottles.

Underline or mark every instance of a name for deity that you encounter as you read the Book of Mormon together as a family. Read how missionaries and advertising students from BYU are using this same technique to help people understand the Book of Mormon better.

https://magazine.byu.edu/article/an-experiment-upon-the-word/

Underline or mark every instance of a name for deity that you encounter as you read the Book of Mormon together as a family. Read how missionaries and advertising students from BYU are using this same technique to help people understand the Book of Mormon better.

https://magazine.byu.edu/article/an-experiment-upon-the-word/

Underline or mark every instance of a name for deity that you encounter as you read the Book of Mormon together as a family. Read how missionaries and advertising students from BYU are using this same technique to help people understand the Book of Mormon better.

https://magazine.byu.edu/article/an-experiment-upon-the-word/

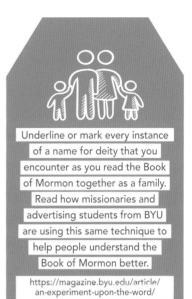

Underline or mark every instance of a name for deity that you encounter as you read the Book of Mormon together as a family. Read how missionaries and advertising students from BYU are using this same technique to help people understand the Book of Mormon better.

https://magazine.byu.edu/article/an-experiment-upon-the-word/

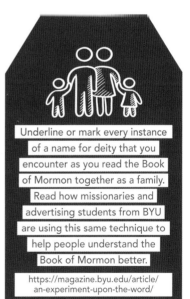

Underline or mark every instance of a name for deity that you encounter as you read the Book of Mormon together as a family. Read how missionaries and advertising students from BYU are using this same technique to help people understand the Book of Mormon better.

https://magazine.byu.edu/article/an-experiment-upon-the-word/

Family Scriptures—Suggested gift: A paperback copy of the Book of Mormon and a scripture highlighting pencil.

You'll use this binder and the list included inside to gather all of the important documents your family needs to store in a safe place (birth certificates, insurance policies, passports and more).

You'll use this binder and the list included inside to gather all of the important documents your family needs to store in a safe place (birth certificates, insurance policies, passports and more).

You'll use this binder and the list included inside to gather all of the important documents your family needs to store in a safe place (birth certificates, insurance policies, passports and more).

You'll use this binder and the list included inside to gather all of the important documents your family needs to store in a safe place (birth certificates, insurance policies, passports and more).

You'll use this binder and the list included inside to gather all of the important documents your family needs to store in a safe place (birth certificates, insurance policies, passports and more).

You'll use this binder and the list included inside to gather all of the important documents your family needs to store in a safe place (birth certificates, insurance policies, passports and more).

Important Documents—Suggested Gift: A 3-ring-binder.

Use this album to print and display your twenty most precious family photos. Then add at least one precious family photo each year. Make sure these photos are saved digitally as well (consider adding them to FamilySearch.org).

Use this album to print and display your twenty most precious family photos. Then add at least one precious family photo each year. Make sure these photos are saved digitally as well (consider adding them to FamilySearch.org).

Use this album to print and display your twenty most precious family photos. Then add at least one precious family photo each year. Make sure these photos are saved digitally as well (consider adding them to FamilySearch.org).

Use this album to print and display your twenty most precious family photos. Then add at least one precious family photo each year. Make sure these photos are saved digitally as well (consider adding them to FamilySearch.org).

Use this album to print and display your twenty most precious family photos. Then add at least one precious family photo each year. Make sure these photos are saved digitally as well (consider adding them to FamilySearch.org).

Use this album to print and display your twenty most precious family photos. Then add at least one precious family photo each year. Make sure these photos are saved digitally as well (consider adding them to FamilySearch.org).

Our Twenty Most Important Family Photographs—
Suggested gift: A small photo album and a thumb drive.